Animal Body Parts

Fish
Body Parts

Clare Lewis

raintree
a Capstone company — publishers for children

Raintree is an imprint of Capstone Global Library Limited, a company incorporated in England and Wales having its registered office at 7 Pilgrim Street, London, EC4V 6LB – Registered company number: 6695582

www.raintree.co.uk
myorders@raintree.co.uk

Edited by Helen Cox Cannons and Shelly Lyons
Designed by Steve Mead
Picture research by Svetlana Zhurkin
Production by Victoria Fitzgerald
Originated by Capstone Global Library Ltd
Printed and bound in China

ISBN 978 1 406 29804 8
19 18 17 16 15
10 9 8 7 6 5 4 3 2 1

British Library Cataloguing in Publication Data
A full catalogue record for this book is available from the British Library.

Acknowledgements
We would like to thank the following for permission to reproduce photographs: We would like to thank the following for permission to reproduce photographs: Dreamstime: Deborah Coles, back cover (left), 11, Dennis Jacobsen, 22 (bottom), Dieter Decroos, 9, Mangroove, 14, Mikhailg, cover (bottom), Miro69, cover (top left), Ryszard Laskowski, 12; Getty Images: Doug Perrine, 22 (middle); Minden Pictures: Alan James, 10, Norbert Wu, 18; Shutterstock: ACEgan, 22 (top), Antonio Martin, 17, assistant, 23 (bubbles), bbevren, 15, 23, Beth Swanson, 8, Ernie Hounshell, 20, Jack Ammit, 16, Joanne Weston, 5, 23, Joe Belanger, 7, Kletr, cover (top right), LauraD, 23 (algae), Meister Photos, 23 (coral), Nantawat Chotsuwan, 6, red-feniks, cover (top middle), Rich Carey, 4, 13, Studio 37, 19, Vlad61, back cover (right), 21.

We would like to thank Michael Bright for his invaluable help in the preparation of this book.

Every effort has been made to contact copyright holders of material reproduced in this book. Any omissions will be rectified in subsequent printings if notice is given to the publisher.

Contents

Some words are shown in bold, **like this**. You can find out what they mean by looking in the glossary.

What is a fish?

Fish live and breathe under water. Most fish have scales and fins.

A sardine is a fish. A shark is a fish, too.

Fish do not all look the same. Their bodies
can be very different from each other.

Let's take a look at parts of their bodies.

Eyes

Fish often have big eyes to help them see underwater.

Most fish have eyes on the sides of their head. They can see all around them.

Flatfish have both eyes on one side. These eyes help the flatfish see upwards when it is lying on the sea floor.

Ears and nostrils

lateral line

Fish have ears inside their heads. We cannot see them. Fish have a line that runs down their bodies, called a lateral line. It helps fish to sense movements.

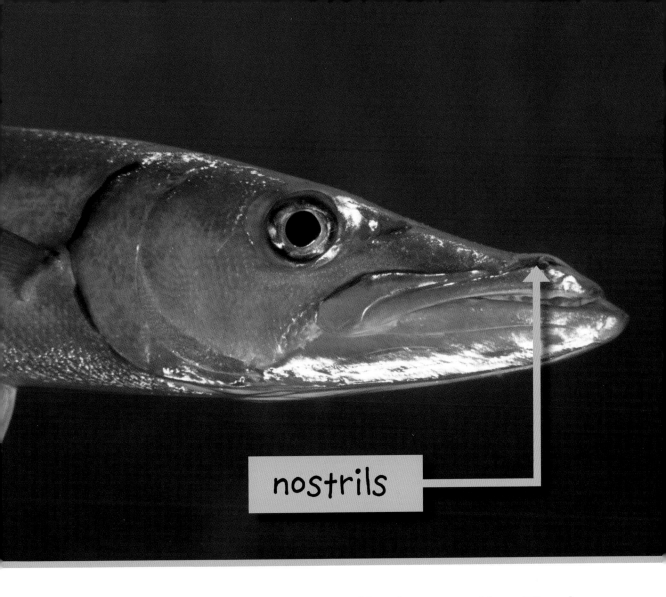

nostrils

Fish have nostrils above their mouths. Their nostrils are for smelling food and other fish.

This barracuda can smell **prey** from far away.

Mouths

Some fish have big mouths.

The basking shark swims with its huge mouth open. It takes in lots of water. It eats the tiny plants and animals in the water.

moray eel

Some eels have two sets of jaws. They bite small fish with their first jaws. Then the second set of jaws pulls the **prey** down the eel's throat.

Teeth

Some fish have lots of pointed teeth. They use their teeth to grab **prey**.

This piranha's teeth are sharp. They are good for holding and tearing flesh.

Parrotfish have beaks as well as teeth.

They use their beaks and teeth to scrape
and crunch **algae**. Algae grow on **coral**
and rocks.

Scales and gills

Most fish have scales. Scales protect their soft bodies. Scales also allow them to move and bend.

Some fish have very colourful skin underneath their scales.

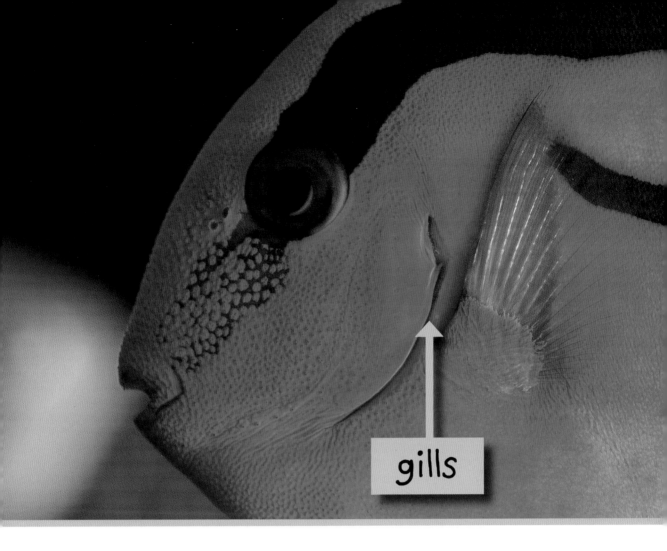

gills

Most fish do not breathe air. They get the **oxygen** they need from the water.

Water enters the fish through the mouth and passes back out through the **gills**.

Fins

fins

Most fish have seven fins. Some fins help the fish swim fast.

Some fins help fish steer through water. Other fins keep fish from rolling over as they swim.

fins

This blenny uses its fins like fingers. The fins hold on to rocks in rough seas.

Some fish, such as mudskippers, use their fins like legs. They can even walk on land.

Tails

tail fin

Most fish have tail fins that help them move quickly through water.

The shape of this swordfish's tail helps it swim very fast.

Seahorses look different from other fish. They have long tails and snouts.

Seahorses wrap their tails around **corals** or seagrasses to stop themselves floating away.

Spines

Some fish have spines to help keep them safe.

This pufferfish swallows water when in danger. It then puffs up into a ball and sticks out its spines.

Lionfish spines are like long needles.

They stab liquid poison, called venom, into their **prey**.

Totally amazing fish body parts!

Jawfishes carry their eggs in their mouths. The eggs are safe there until the baby fish hatch.

An angler fish has a special type of fin that sticks out of its head. It has a light on the end of it. The light attracts **prey**.

Lungfish can live out of water for years at a time. They have a lung as well as **gills**.

Glossary

algae plant-like living things that grow in the sea

coral hard, stony substance made from skeletons of dead sea creatures

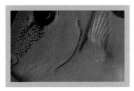

gills parts of the body that let animals breathe under water

oxygen gas that all animals need to live

prey animal that is hunted by another animal

Find out more

Books

Fish (Animal Classifications), Angela Royston
(Raintree, 2015)
Why Do Salmon and Other Fish Have Scales? (Animal Body
Coverings), Holly Beaumont (Raintree, 2015)

Websites

Learn about more amazing fish at:
animals.nationalgeographic.com/animals/fish

Find wonderful photographs and watch videos all about
fish at:
www.bbc.co.uk/nature/animals/by/fish

Index